Honorable Assets

A Beginner's Guide To The World Of
Cryptocurrency

Taariq Paul A.K.A Cryptoreek
William Sanchez, Jr. A.K.A ThysirPips

Dedication

Taariq: *I dedicate this to my beautiful wife, Basia, my gorgeous daughter Nevaeh and my handsome son, Joaquin.*

William: *For my two boys, Abel and William, who keep me going on this roller coaster called life.*

CONTENTS

Introduction

The market cap of cryptocurrencies reached 2.1 trillion U.S. dollars from less than 1 trillion in 2021. To put this into perspective, the total market cap of all health-food-related businesses worldwide has not yet reached a trillion dollars. That is the immense value of cryptocurrencies.

Multiple people out there have made millions from trading in crypto. The market for crypto-currencies is so much more volatile than the stock market and traditional forms of trading and investing that they regularly give a thousand (even more) times the return on investments.

However, a much larger contingent of people has lost massive amounts trying to trade in this market. The unfortunate reality of this world is that many investors are not familiar with how the market works and end up losing their investments on coins that should not be considered in the first place. A cautionary tale is a recent crash in Terra and Luna's coins experienced by one of the most significant communities involved in cryptocurrency since Bitcoin. In the latter parts of this book, we will look further into other examples of people getting into this world without a proper understanding of what it is and getting burnt as a result.

Without proper research, cryptocurrency can make you feel like Alice falling down the rabbit hole. Even though the term "cryptocurrency" and even "NFTs" have become incredibly familiar in the last decade, not many people understand what they mean. And this is not without a need either. The technology involved in this world is quite complex and entertains ideas that need to be discussed on a higher level. People with only a surface-level knowledge of these things tend to make many mistakes with their learning.

This is simply how most things are in this modern world, unfortunately.

There is a lot of information available at the touch of your hands. Still, the act of vetting the information available and extracting practical learning from it is a matter much more complicated than advertised. We have not evolved to look through so much information. Instead, humans are more accustomed to lighter, shallower ideas because that kind of data is more pertinent to our survival than more significant data points. And so, memes are lighter and travel farther than heavier, more "rigorously learned" ideas as they put it in the world of mathematics. But I digress.

Every article or blog relating to these topics is filled with terms like "decentralized finance," "blockchain," and many other intimidating phrases that can scare away the novices. These complexities act as barriers to entry for prospective investors, and thankfully the whole point of this book is to break down these barriers.

We hope that with our help, anyone with the right mindset and eagerness to learn can become an expert in the world of cryptocurrency.

Also, there are functionalities to this kind of technology that have not been properly explored, at least in the mainstream, or talked about in popular media. There is much more to the world of cryptocurrencies and NFTs than just as an asset to trade for profit. The latter aspect tends to overshadow all the practical uses for the incredible technology in play here.

By the end of this book, readers will develop a deeper understanding of cryptocurrency the products available in the cryptocurrency space, and more.

Before taking the first step, you should know that we are not financial advisors. This handbook is purely for educational purposes. We cannot turn anyone into a millionaire. Only you can make yourself rich; we provide you with all the necessary tools to get you there. The framework for discerning the information you receive will be provided in this book. The decision-making processes and the more subtle changes in the market are things that no one can teach or predict.

Most importantly, you cannot go into this expecting to become a professional overnight. As the famous idiom states, Rome was not built in a day. And even though many crypto-millionaires do become so over short periods, you cannot expect to do so without learning about the field. Unless you just get fortunate, of course.

This field takes time, practice, and patience to perfect. So, go easy on yourself and have fun with it as you continue to learn and grow.

Chapter 1: Bitcoin

So, let us begin this book with the million-dollar question: *What is cryptocurrency?*

To fully answer that, we need to dissect and thoroughly examine the most popular of the cryptocurrencies — **Bitcoin**.

Bitcoin is the first cryptocurrency created in 2009 by someone known only by their alias, Satoshi Nakamoto. But we need to back it up to explain this emergence into the mainstream fully. The first thing in this series of events was publishing a White Paper—The Bitcoin White Paper. "What exactly is a White Paper?" I hear you asking. A White Paper is a document companies issue when introducing a new product into the market. Especially in the case of new technologies, these White Papers serve as informational documents that explain what the product does and what kind of market it will serve. It serves as an introduction to a new product or service.

This White Paper, issued on the 31st of October, 2008, was so impactful that Jack Dorsey, the C.E.O. of Twitter, claimed that this was a seminal piece of work in computer science for the last three decades. But what did it entail? It proposed a system that would solve the problem of having a decentralized financial system.

Referred to as the Byzantine Fault, one of the biggest problems for any computer scientist developing a decentralized financial system is bypassing the need for intermediaries. How would two peers conduct business online without involving a neutral third party? And of course, all intermediaries are subject to take their cuts or take the information of these transactions and watch over your every move.

The White Paper provided the proof of concept for the technology that could solve this problem (blockchain). Afterward, Bitcoin became the first currency that relied on the blockchain to make payments secure, trackable, and transparent, yet keep the people doing these transactions anonymous and their identities safe. This was one of the most impactful pieces of technology in the last few decades, and, of course, we have already delved a little into the current market cap of the industry that such an invention eventually spawned.

So, what exactly is the value that this technology provides? To reiterate, these transactions are public information and, for the most part, anonymous and can be made without brokers or intermediaries. Usually, the broker or intermediary is any third party that ensures that the transaction occurs and there is an agreement between the two parties involved in the exchange.

Without an intermediary, the validity of a transaction between two parties can be questioned by either of them. This would cause the trust in the transaction medium to drop and not work in the future. As mentioned before, the drawbacks of intermediaries are both monetary and privacy-based. If you do not want banks or other services (like PayPal) to know your business, then the only alternative is to go the crypto-route. I mean, it's in the name, isn't it? The 'crypto' part comes from the Greek word "Kryptos," which means "hidden."

Despite being a digital currency, Bitcoin can still be used to buy tangible goods. In its nascent stages, it was associated with crimes like money laundering, drug trafficking, and even sex trafficking.

This was typical since there was no way that government agencies could monitor transactions or take their cut. Intermediaries that relish the ideas of centralized finance and keep their eyes on everyone did not want this to happen, especially regarding money. The digital asset has shed some of that early reputation as a currency for the black market and has come a long way towards legitimacy.

You can buy anything from luxury watches, average consumer commodities, and even your insurance with cryptocurrencies. Major crypto-exchanges provide debit cards attached to your crypto-wallets, and these can function as regular debit cards that you can use to withdraw money and buy products or services.

Bitcoin is also decentralized. This means it isn't controlled by a bank or government system either. It is considered a peer-to-peer transaction model. That means that there are no third parties involved in the transactions that take place.

Blockchain makes this crypto asset work smoothly, essentially a digital ledger that promotes transparency, accountability, and trust. Anyone can access and view the details of transactions made to and from crypto-wallets, but the wallets themselves are not linked to anyone's identities. Instead of having a single ledger in control of the intermediary that could or could not mess with these records, the log is easy to access and view but impossible to mess with and edit. The whole idea of there being cryptocurrencies in the first place is built upon the concepts and technology of the blockchain.

Bitcoin is now a legalized tender in El Salvador, adopted by members of the United States Congress, and is now one of the most queried assets in the stock market. During the 2022 Super Bowl, cryptocurrency commercials made up around 40% of all ad revenues. So, why would anyone want to use this? Well, we'll first have to understand how money works. Money is a concept of stored value. However, what people consider valuable enough to use or exchange is considered money. The paper currency that we know today works because it is assigned value. It used to be backed up as legal tender by gold. But that's no longer the case. The problem with these currencies is that they are centralized and subject to the Central Bank's whim (read, government). The government decides to print more or less money, and their decisions influence the value of your currency. Traditional money is inflatable and has lost 40% of its value since March 2020 due to COVID-19. Inflation is a problem Bitcoin and cryptocurrency are here to fix.

Unlike money printed daily, only a finite amount of Bitcoin will be available. All Bitcoin is expected to be mined by the year 2140. The way this becomes available is through a process called mining. Having a finite amount of Bitcoin allows the price to increase over time. Once the supply is gone, the demand will be through the roof. To keep this digital asset deflationary, Bitcoin goes through halving every four years, when the rewards miners get are cut in half.

In the world of cryptocurrency, Bitcoin is considered 'digital gold.' It is not only the first digital currency in existence but also an asset with the most significant market cap, currently holding a market dominance of 42%.

One thing that is now clear is that Bitcoin is here to stay.

Chapter 2: Alt Coins

The unfortunate reality of a financial instrument or any asset that reaches mainstream acclaim is that making money through it becomes more difficult. Thankfully, Bitcoin and other mainstream coins remain volatile despite mainstream acclaim.

Since everyone and their mums know what Coca-Cola is, you are less likely to profit significantly from its stock. This is because Coca-Cola is, in the financial world, "priced in." Since most of the players in the market now know the value of Coke or will be in the future (roughly, of course), the asking rate right now for Coca-Cola does not justify the selling price later.

The most mainstream of the cryptocurrencies is Bitcoin. It was easy to make money off Bitcoin a few years ago, but you must be pretty competent to make a profit. Let us look at Bitcoin's value over the last few years.

In 2015, about seven years ago, you could have bought a single Bitcoin without a second thought. Around that time, one whole Bitcoin was worth around 350–400 USD. Bitcoin was well-known but not as much as it became later on. This was perhaps the best time to buy Bitcoin because it was nowhere near priced. In 2017, Bitcoin reached around 20,000 USD before dropping and staying low for another few years. The most prominent peak happened in 2021 when it reached the unprecedented price of about 65,000 USD.

Even though it is now a bit more challenging to make money off of crypto, it is still possible. You can buy fractional amounts of Bitcoin or ether if a whole coin is too expensive. But some more currencies are quite a bit more volatile than both of the leading crypto. These are for those that are looking to make a lot more money than more stable coins or other financial instruments.

There are more and more currencies being minted in the crypto-world. There is a lesser chance of these kinds of currencies being priced in. Many people getting rich off crypto-trading are now dealing with these coins.

Crypto-currencies of this type are known as Altcoins or alternate coins, such as Ethereum, B.N.B., X.R.P., or Solana. Altcoins carry the same premise as Bitcoin, utilizing the same kind of blockchain technology.

Additionally, they try to implement improvements they perceive as flaws in Bitcoin mining, value structure, or other lacunae. Ethereum, for example, seized an opportunity beyond just financial transactions. It utilizes blockchain to record agreements in intelligent contracts, believing that they will soon be able to cut out the costly middleman one would encounter when dealing with banks, insurance, and copyright companies. To elaborate further, where Bitcoin was made for the express purpose of decentralized finance (we will get into that in more detail later on), Ethereum had a different meaning altogether. Ethereum was designed to enable contracts and apps.

Well, what does this mean?

Inspired by Bitcoin in 2009, Vitalik Buterin co-founded Ethereum with the help of crowdfunding in 2014. The currency was set up to enable the second largest crypto-currency to date, ether. Instead of relying on the technology behind Bitcoin, Ether relies on smart contracts to guarantee that the transactions happening are transparent and fast.

Another use for Ethereum is as a programming language. Since it is open-source and the ledger system is distributed across volunteer systems across the globe, it allows for people to use it to make their applications and the like. Ethereum served as the next step after Bitcoin in blockchain technology, and its utility extends beyond being used for currency alone.

13

Unfortunately, Ether had loopholes that allowed for a hack earlier in its heyday, and a hacker was able to make off with about 50 million USD in Ethereum. Other Altcoins proclaim a faster, decentralized, scalable, and cheaper product. Although the world of Altcoins may seem intimidating, with more than 10,000 different coins in circulation, they can be broken down into five categories.

The first category is native crypto, created to run and operate on their blockchains like Bitcoin, Ethereum, or B.N.B. The whole purpose of these kinds of crypto is to function as currency on the blockchain curated for them. For example, Ethereum technology is first made, and the native crypto that operates on the Ethereum technology is ether. So, ether is the native crypto for the Ethereum blockchain.

Another excellent example of an altcoin is Doge-coin. It was set up as a meme-coin after the famed shiba-inu meme. When Elon Musk tweeted about Doge-coin, it shot up and is currently at an all-time low, with no real future rises. Still, the technology behind Doge-coin is pretty sound, despite there being high volatility.

The next category is tokens. These value units operate on an existing blockchain and can only be used for specific purposes within that environment. Where coins are used for transactions alone, tokens are used for much more. They are kept as a store of value (assets) and for trading and serve as a kind of investment tool for people by functioning as an asset.

Next, we have Stablecoins. Stablecoins were developed to offer the advantages of cryptocurrencies and tokens without price volatility. They accomplish this by tying their value to an existing currency, 1:1. Tether, the largest Stablecoin, is linked to the U.S dollar; therefore, one tether will always be equivalent to one U.S dollar. You don't buy stable coins for a profit. They are used to hold value for making other cryptocurrency purchases in a bear market. A Stablecoin is like the gold or government bond of the crypto-world. They do not allow one to risk a lot to make a significant profit, but they will enable one to have currency ready to trade to buy the dip at an opportune moment. You sell at the peak, transfer your crypto into a Stablecoin, and convert it back into more volatile cryptos at their lowest point for a future profit.

Our next category is forks. Forks happen whenever a community makes a change to the blockchain protocol. There are two types of forks—a soft fork and a hard fork. A soft fork is when new features or functions occur on the programming level. This is just a change in the blockchain software; as long as everyone decides to go along with this change, this makes it the new version of the older coin. Hard forks occur when the entire code is changed, and most old processes sometimes become obsolete. Bitcoin Cash and Gold are newer currencies spawned off of Bitcoin and result from forks.

The last category is meme coins, a.k.a 'shit coins.'

As the name suggests, these coins are based on a joke with little to no utility. Crypto influencers try to capitalize on short-term gains with high volatility in these projects. They are usually short-lived and over-hyped. Many of these meme coins end up in a rug pull. A rug pull is nothing different than a kind of pyramid scheme. The creators of these will market these kinds of currencies to the public through discord servers, subreddits, and social media influencers. They then wait for the hype to build until many people buy into the coins and cause the value of these coins to rise. Then, when the value has increased, the creators and early investors pull out and mass-sell all the coins they held. They take all the value the new investors provide by investing and stealing their money.

An excellent example is the "Save the Kids" coin marketed through the P.R. power-house FaZe and some other internet celebrities. Be extra careful when investing in projects like these. Shit coins are nothing more than a gamble, and they can only be invested in the same way you would buy a ticket for the lottery.

Familiarizing yourself with Altcoins will help you understand the functionalities of new emerging coins. It also allows you to look beyond Bitcoin, find familiarity with different projects, and decide on what you believe in.

Remember: it is always in your best interest to do your research and have a genuine interest in the project you're investing in. Understanding market caps and market dominance will also be vital in identifying new or potential Altcoins to invest in.

But we must look beyond just making money regarding cryptocurrencies and the blockchain. The significant part of Ethereum was that it allowed people to experiment with the technology to create new tools based on its technology.

Furthermore, we must be extra-cautious when we think about investing or trusting our stable assets to be stored as crypto. Even Stablecoins that are theoretically safe from dips in value are very susceptible (especially recently) to crashes. An excellent example is a recent disaster with Terra and Luna, two coins tied to Stablecoins and crashed in value within a week.

Also, if your wallet is a hot wallet (connected to the internet), it is wise to funnel the currency from this kind of wallet to a cold wallet. The latter is a much safer choice since it is less vulnerable to hacks and is not accessible to people over the internet.

Another suitable methodology for keeping your investment safe is to have multiple wallets. This distributes your risk since having one wallet would allow the hacker to perform one hack to access all of your cryptos.

Stay safe, trade smart, and continuously diversify.

Chapter 3: Decentralized Finance

Now the main principle behind the establishment of the foundation of the blockchain and the crypto-world is decentralizing finance. Most of us have heard of this term by now, and many of us that have even slightly dipped our toes in the crypto-world are aware of the phrase "DEFI" or Decentralized Finance. But what exactly does it mean, and why is it of so much importance in the world of modern virtual currency? This makes for a little history lesson and a dive into what centralized finance is and why decentralized finance is such an important buzzword.

The History of Centralized Finance

Centralized finance stretches back to the beginnings of human civilization. Even ancient Mesopotamia boasted a system of centralized finance, and it is thought that they were the first ones to come up with a system such as that. Humans employed centralized finance when the barter system was still in play, and things like cattle and tools were used as currency. Then came precious metals, and the transition into the modern era was completed when currency became the fiat currency we know today. Governments across the globe back legal tender.

The basis of a centralized system is a government or similar entity with the might to back the system. Governments have armies and procedures to guarantee that the system remains (relatively) stable with laws prohibiting such systems' destabilization. This was born out of necessity since carrying around precious metals is a difficult task, and guaranteeing that the currency you hold in one place is valued the same in another was impossible without a centralized system back in the day. Thus, we had currencies of imputed value rather than intrinsic value.

This was the solution to the problem of keeping transactions stable and secure since a trader in the market, and the buyer were both aware of the value of a coin. If one or both were frivolous with this, the city guard would be called upon to make them comply.

Now, unfortunately, there are problems with having these intermediaries.

The Need for Decentralization

First: since your transaction is being secured by the intermediary (bank, financial corporation, payment app), they are privy to the identities of the ones doing the transaction and are aware of what is going on between what two parties. Having the government or other intermediaries know your business might rub you the wrong way. There is no guaranteed privacy when it comes to transactions.

Now this is not just a concern for your libertarian "crazy" uncle, it concerns us all.

Having the government or big corporation keep such an intense eye on you is uncomfortable, to say the least. Plus, with big corporations, they can sell your details around and you can find yourself in a barrage of targeted ads and recommendations that no one likes. The more surveilled our activities become, the closer we get to a dark dystopian reality like the one portrayed in the book 1984.

Second: the intermediary takes his cut. Either you pay taxes to the government or fees to the app that you are using to complete said transaction. These things most certainly have to happen whenever we involve third parties in things like these.

Third: most importantly, the control of the value of currencies is not in the hand of the currency holder. It is strictly down to the government to control the flow of the currency and determine its value that way. Take the recent example of what happened in Afghanistan. The currency's value increases or decreases based on factors outside the individual's control. That is how things are.

Benefits of Decentralization in Finance

With this comes the advent of Decentralized Finance. Novel imputed currencies have come out and these do not require the permission, the interruption, or need of a third party. These currencies are not dependent upon institutions keeping secretive records but are maintained on publicly available ledgers and open to the public.

This means there is assured transparency while also maintaining the identities of the entities involved in transactions anonymous if they choose to do so. The records of wallets are publicly accessible, but the holders of these wallets are not a matter of public record. Two unknown parties can have a safe and secure transaction with these ledgers without the government's interception.

What this means is, your crazy uncle can pay for his everyday needs to be delivered to him without having to worry about the government, or anyone else, knowing or taking their cut.

Most importantly, the currency backed by a decentralized financial system gives the asset holder the most control over any other intermediary.

If your assets are in a bank, the government can quickly freeze them, destroy them, and prevent them from being transferred.

Decentralized Finance, better known as DEFI, is a financial world comprised of decentralized and non-custodial financial technologies. These techniques include exchanges, lending/borrowing protocols, incubation of new products, yield farming, staking, and much more. While these terms may seem daunting to absorb, they're pretty simple once broken down.

How does DEFI Work?

Let's start with a decentralized exchange or DEX. This is a peer-to-peer marketplace where transactions occur directly between crypto traders. There is no third party involved.

DEXs can fulfill one of cryptocurrency's core possibilities: fostering financial transactions that aren't officiated by banks, brokers, payment processors, or any other intermediary.

The most popular DEXs, like Uniswap and PancakeSwap, utilize the Ethereum and Binance blockchain and are a part of the growing suite of DEFI tools.

This makes many financial services available directly from a compatible crypto-wallet like Metamask. It is important to remember that decentralized exchanges do not exchange other currencies for crypto, just crypto for other cryptos. You have to buy cryptocurrencies yourself before trying to trade here.

So what can one do with cryptocurrency?

Crypto-Lending

Crypto lending is similar to the concept of traditional lending. The only difference is that you would be lending different types of Cryptocurrencies to borrowers instead of fiat currency, otherwise known as government-backed currency.

Investors who lend their crypto to borrowers on a decentralized platform get interest payments. These payments are also called "crypto-dividends." Several platforms allow users to not only lend cryptocurrencies but also accept Stablecoins.

Launchpads/ Incubators

Another essential DEFI term you should become familiar with is Launchpad. Launchpads, or incubators, are platforms that allow blockchain-based projects to raise capital while giving access to early-stage token sales for their group of investors.

These incubators are usually membership-based and give investors early access to sales at a bargain price before being publicly launched. Launchpads are known for their marketing of a project to raise awareness. These projects are highly volatile and are not for the faint of heart. Remember that though a launchpad allows you access to a project early, this does not guarantee success.

DAOs

Decentralized Autonomous Organizations or D.A.O.s are community-led entities with no central authority. They are fully independent and transparent with intelligent contracts that lay the foundational rules.

They execute the agreed-upon decisions, and, at any point, they can propose, vote, and even have the code publicly audited. A DAO is governed entirely by its members, who collectively make critical decisions about the future of a project.

Some of these decisions could be technical upgrades, treasury allocations, or the project's future. A core team of community members establishes the rules of the D.A.O. through intelligent contracts.

These contracts lay the foundation on which the D.A.O. is to operate. They are evident, verifiable, and publicly auditable to ensure that any potential member can fully understand how the protocol functions.

Yield Farming

Yield farming is a process that allows shareholders to lock up their holdings which provides them with rewards. This process will enable investors to earn fixed or variable interest by investing crypto in a DEFI market.

Simply put, yield farming involves lending crypto via a blockchain. When banks make loans using fiat, they are paid back with interest. The same is true with yield farming. If you store your cryptocurrency in a DEX, it is best to consider utilizing it in a yield farming venture as it provides liquidity and rewards.

Staking Crypto

The last term we'll discuss in this chapter is staking. This is the act of committing assets to a blockchain network. By engaging your assets, you're allowing transactions to be validated. The more assets committed to the network, the stronger it becomes. Stakeholders receive interest determined by the amount they stake. The APY can range from eight to twenty percent for more established projects. Some newer and riskier projects can vary from eighty to one hundred percent APY.

The main difference between staking and yield farming is that you don't have to pair the token with equal liquidity with staking.

In Conclusion

The world of DEFI may seem complex, but you will find that it is similar to a bank and the products they offer with enough research. This is the sole concept that has to be drilled into the hearts and minds of anyone interested in the world of crypto and to begin investing in this new technology.

Before committing to an investment, you must know your risk. You must weigh it against the returns you can get and then make your investments accordingly.

While there are many benefits to decentralized finance, there are downfalls to using a system with no middle man to protect your funds as you risk losing money with no insurance. If you are defrauded, you cannot make a call and freeze the transaction like you would if you made an accidental transaction or were defrauded via credit card. It is essential to be careful when using your hot wallet and keeping your passwords secure.

Perhaps the best way forwards would be to have a system incorporating the good things of both systems. If there were to be a system of decentralized finance that would also allow for a safeguard against being defrauded and bad transactions, then that would become the primary system being used.

This is why it is crucial to be diligent and always conduct your research before investing in any projects in DEFI.

Chapter 4: NFTs

If you're reading this, you've probably come across the term NFTs. Mostly from crypto "bros" that do not know what they are talking about, but I digress. NFTs are spoken in the same sentences as Bitcoin and other cryptocurrencies and are seen more as investment tools than valued for the incredible technology that enables their existence. And it makes sense too. NFTs have made multiple headlines, featuring the obscene amounts of money involved in their sale and trading. Incredible art-works have been made into NFTs and sold online to the highest bidders, bringing in millions of dollars. So let us look at what NFTs are and what the world of NFTs has been and might be in the future.

To be straightforward NFT stands for Non-Fungible Tokens. Fungible means interchangeable. NFTs show full ownership of a product which is verified through the blockchain. NFTs can represent ownership in almost anything, from digital art to virtual real estate. Much like how the blockchain enables records to be kept safely and transparently for crypto, these online ledgers and contracts can make virtual ownership much safer than ever. A real-world painting is verified through its history, records, and "genealogy" of where it was and where it is.

This occurs virtually for NFTs, so anyone can verify whether artist X made a particular piece of art or not. And if the person owned it, you were buying it from. Reducing the probability of "let me sell you a bridge" type deals.

It has often proved challenging to demonstrate rights in the digital asset space. Anyone could crop a picture they found online and then claim they made/bought it. But with the introduction of NFTs, demonstrating ownership has been revolutionized.

Contrary to Bitcoin or dollars, NFTs are described as non-fungible because each is unique and has its value. For example, a dollar can be exchanged for another with no problem. But a Rembrandt cannot be valued the same as a Picasso or the stick figures you drew on your school desk as a child. A fungible token can be exchanged, one for the other, retaining value. A non-fungible ticket is valued on an individual basis.

In 2021, this new type of art technology and investment tool emerged onto the finance and art scene with the record Christie's sale of Beeple's Everyday: The First 5000 Days NFT for almost seventy million dollars. This phenomenon has started to make real waves much later than Bitcoin and other cryptos, nearly a decade after Bitcoin became mainstream, but they have been around for quite a while.

In 2012, a paper by Meni Rosenfield was made public, introducing the 'Colored Coins' concept for the blockchain. The idea of Colored Coins was to theorize methods for connecting real-world assets on the blockchain to prove ownership of those assets, similar to regular Bitcoins, but with an added element that determines their use, making them unique and individual.

The limitations of blockchain technology at the time meant that the colored coins concept could never be realized; however, it spearheaded the chain of ideas that led to the creation of NFTs a couple of years later.

Digital artist Kevin McCoy minted the first-known NFT 'Quantum' on the Name coin blockchain. 'Quantum' is hailed as the first ever true NFT. A piece of digital art that could be safely owned by an individual and could be verified by anyone. This revolutionized the world of digital art, and artists could no longer have to worry about piracy or their work being taken credit for.

The real, meaningful advancement for NFTs was introducing a set of token standards, allowing the creation of tokens by developers. The token standard is a subsidiary of the intelligent contract standard, which includes teaching developers how to make and "publish" new tokens in line with the underlying blockchain technology. This made it easier for more developers to use blockchain technology.

John Watkinson and Matt Hall created "cryptopunks." These were among the first NFTs and were part of an experiment to see what the technology could be used for. The art pieces, inspired by the London Punk scene, were free, and it was just to see how the contracts could be used to verify authenticity.

It was a success; from then on, artists could quickly sell their art online. They did not have to pay to have their art curated, nor did they have to worry about aggressive intermediaries they had to be at the mercy of to sell their work.

2021 became the year of the NFT, and the market cap for the industry skyrocketed like nothing else in the virtual world. One of the most significant factors in this boom was innovations within the art market and the industry at large when Christie's and Sotheby's (a very prestigious auction house and curator) took their auctions into the virtual world and began selling NFT art.

This gave credibility to the virtual art market and the stamp of approval that NFTs needed to skyrocket to what they became soon after.

This led to Christie's record-breaking sale of Beeple's Everyday: the First 5000 Days NFT for millions we mentioned. This was quickly overtaken by other sales of NFTs that crossed the barrier into the hundreds of millions of dollars mark. The skyrocketing demand for NFTs resulted from the Christie's auction; another knock-on effect was other blockchains getting involved and starting their versions of NFTs. Innovations are often made when people see what is possible, and there is an incentive to do so.

These included blockchains such as Solana, Tezos, and Flow. With these newer platforms for NFTs, some new standards were established to ensure the authenticity and uniqueness of digital assets. Towards the end of the year, once Facebook rebranded as Meta and moved into the Metaverse, NFTs became mainstream.

Because no two NFTs are alike, they're impossible to falsify. So, how do you make money with an NFT?

These days, you can trade N.B.A. trading cards through N.B.A. Top-shot or buy and sell blue-chip NFTs like the Bored Ape Yacht Club on the Opensea marketplace.

NFT buyers often look for rarity in projects as a status symbol. Much like art in the real world, you would want to own a Picasso and have ownership and originality verified by experts and art enthusiasts. Now, these people can buy and own art that they can have online and whose authenticity could be verified by anyone that wishes to do so. NFTs like these could hold value better since they could not be faked. In the real world, art collectors always worry about damage or fakes. They do not have to do so when it comes to NFTs.

In contrast, others look for a utility like exclusive memberships, airdrops, Metaverse (a virtual universe), real estate, and many other opportunities. Shortly after the Metaverse is at its peak, you can see NFTs being utilized heavily. People could own digital mansions and keep the digital art they own inside them without fear of these being stolen or anything happening to them. Even if these digital assets are copied, it does not matter since anyone can distinguish the fake from the original with a few buttons, checking online ledgers to see where it came from and where it went regarding ownership.

However, the actual utility in NFTs will likely show true ownership of high-value items, transfer ownership of valuable items without intermediaries, contractual agreements, or even a completely free commerce market, especially for the arts communities.

To reiterate, for the longest time, artists themselves have had to go through multiple intermediaries to have a hope of having a chance at having their work monetized and being able to have a livable earning. Art collectors would go to curations and shows to pick out what they wanted or bid on a piece of art and still have to worry about damage, the art being fake, and much more. With NFTs, artists and art collectors can benefit, cutting out the middle man. Furthermore, NFTs can be used to verify the authenticity of club memberships, concert tickets, and many other things where it is helpful to have digital assets that cannot be falsified.

Whichever way you see fit to dip your toes into the vast waters of NFTs, there are specific terms you will need to become familiar with before you dive in.

The first term is Web 3.0. This is decentralized internet surfing in a nutshell. The days of logging in with a username and password were considered Web 2.0, whereas Web3 simply logged in with only your wallet address. Popular Web3 browsers include Metamask, Trust Wallet, and Phantom Wallet. Your identity remains anonymous, but your purchasing ability is alive and well.

Minting is another term to be aware of. This converts a digital file or asset into a crypto collectible or adds it to a blockchain for verification or sale. You may also come across the term gas fees. Users make payments to compensate for the computing energy required to process and validate transactions on the Ethereum blockchain. Depending on the time, gas fees can be costly, which has caused people in the NFT world to start looking into other chains like Solana to mint and purchase NFTs.

NFTs, without a doubt, will have one of the most robust cases for use in the future, working in tandem with crypto. They will be able to show ownership of digital products and showcase them in the Metaverse without a chance of them being stolen.

However, before getting into NFTs with the idea that one can simply create a picture of a monkey and make millions of dollars, take the time to understand what an NFT is and why it can be helpful for you and the cryptocurrency space. YouTube and Google are your best friends when researching new NFT projects, but it doesn't hurt to look at a project's Twitter, Telegram, and Medium page to see how big or anticipated the project is.

Most projects you look at may be on the Ethereum blockchain, but the gas fees are insanely high, so it may be in your best interest to start exploring NFTs on other networks such as Solana, Binance, and Tezos; their gas fees are a fraction of the cost. When it comes to NFTs, don't look to get rich quickly. Look to get rich safely. This is true for all kinds of investments in the virtual space.

Also, there is a tremendous amount of scope for developers to use this technology for new products and pieces of technology, so it might be worthwhile to invest in research companies looking to do so. They might be creating the next big thing and solving massive problems in the online and virtual space.

An excellent example of this is the rise in NFTs in the gaming sphere, where monetization for developers has become incredibly easy. Triple A.A.A. gaming has been on the downfall with the emergence of Moba and Gamba, but the NFT technology has made it so that owning virtual assets (like skins and maps) can serve as a tip system for gamers. They can buy a sixty-dollar game and then choose to "tip" the developers via buying NFT skins that can be transferable outside the game itself. This revolutionizes the world of microtransactions by making them far less predatory and more voluntary by providing more control to gamers.

Similarly, smart contracts in NFTs can change other aspects of the online sphere apart from only art. The scope of future money-making opportunities from the industry and technology is immense.

Chapter 5: Exchanges

Now that you better understand cryptocurrencies let's talk about "exchanges."

Before we can dive into what crypto exchanges are and how they function, we should try and understand the core concept of exchanges in the first place. The modern world of crypto-finance is the next step in the evolution of already existing systems. Like crypto was the next step in currency, evolving from fiat into the virtual world, so are these exchanges. But where and why did the first exchanges like these come from?

In the beginning, a caveman wanted berries, and another had some. The second caveman had berries but wanted meat. This, the first one, had. And so, they made the trade. This was how the barter system was established. With time, this trade advanced until people could have a third in-between object to hold value-gold. After this, the trade rose, and things continued until the first companies were established. Now, the owners of these companies needed money to invest in them and so began selling ownership bit by bit to raise funds, sharing the profit.

This practice evolved until the fourteenth century, when Antwerp, what is now known as Belgium, became a center of trade for the entire globe. Here, merchants would buy and keep goods until they could sell them at a higher price in the future.

Two hundred years later, in 1611, the Dutch East India Company became the first publicly traded company. These companies began to sell shares that varied in price. People started selling and buying to profit from the trade rather than the company's profits. This laid the foundation of the stock exchange.

An enterprising group of merchants made what is known as the Buttonwood Tree Agreement. The men would meet daily to buy and sell stocks and bonds, a practice that eventually came to become the New York Stock Exchange.

The Philadelphia Stock Exchange became the first actual stock exchange established to buy and sell stocks. This laid the foundation of most modern stock exchanges, and the activities in these exchanges were done with fiat currency (now virtual, in the contemporary world).

With the advent of virtual currency that was not fiat and did not need governing authorities, a new kind of exchange was needed. This is where C.E.X. or centralized exchanges come in.

Exchanges or centralized exchanges (C.E.X.s) are businesses that use similar modules to stock exchanges.

Though many online exchanges tried to set up with similar ideas to Bitcoin (anonymity, freedom from surveillance, etc.), they were shut down by authorities since they broke many international regulations.

However, the game was changed with the introduction of Bitcoin in 2008. Since Bitcoin is not a fiat currency, the trading of it was not under the supervision of authorities that could then shut it down. This opened the way for exchanges to form based on the principles of freedom and transparency that cryptocurrencies offered.

They allow the conversion of fiat to cryptocurrency. How is that done? These exchanges allowed one to transfer and convert their bank account balance into the crypto of their choice. The currency went to the exchanges, allowing for cryptos to be deposited into the virtual wallets of those that deposited the money.

A CEX is built by a centralized organization company that acts as a third person to store assets, regulate exchanges, and charge exchange fees. The benefit was obvious-it would provide the security of a third party but the transparency and anonymity for the buyer or seller.

In a C.E.X., the exchange process happens via an order book which sets up the price for a specific cryptocurrency based on current buy and sells orders. Similar to where stock prices are listed on the stock exchange, a share of Caterpillar, for example, would have different prices to buy and sell; everyone knows this while they do the transactions. This ensures that there is no problem with people being unaware of the price they are getting versus the price they have to pay to buy a particular asset.

This type of crypto exchange is currently the most popular globally and is typically used by crypto newcomers. C.E.X.s are user-friendly platforms that make purchasing and managing digital currencies extremely simple.

Coinbase, Binance, Gemini, Kraken, and Kucoin are currently the most popular C.E.X.s. Now, there are pros and cons to using centralized exchanges.

Let's start with the pros.

Firstly, you have insurance. This is a gamechanger when it comes to cryptocurrency. Before, if you made a deal to buy from a shady dealer, you would not know if the transfer would be made. Now, things are much safer and more secure.

With C.E.X.s, you can rest assured knowing that your funds will be safe in the instance of a hack.

You also have fiat as you can easily convert your banknotes to cryptocurrency and vice versa, which gives you liquidity as you would always be able to buy or sell. Transactions on a C.E.X. are usually much faster and are incredibly user-friendly, making it a newcomer's first choice. Now that you understand the pros, let's get into the cons.

With a C.E.X., you must know your customer. This means that all centralized exchanges, by law, have to collect some identification and social security numbers from all customers.

You may also run into issues of a transaction declined for various reasons when dealing with different financial institutions, which is an issue you would not encounter on a decentralized exchange. The last point you should consider is that cryptocurrency was started to decentralize finance, with no middlemen, and to have centralized exchanges, which is somewhat contradictory as it is still supervised. But going forwards, this kind of system where the best of both worlds is combined in a hybrid way to improve service will probably win out in the future.

Coinbase and Binance are great options for buying and selling cryptocurrency for a beginner just starting into the crypto space. Cashapp has also become a seamless option for crypto purchases with 1-3% fees. However, at this time, they are only accepting Bitcoin. If you want to make smaller deposits, it may be in your best interest to check out a Bitcoin A.T.M.

While A.T.M. fees are very high, you can enjoy some anonymity if you stay under a certain amount. Unfortunately, nowadays, it's highly likely that you will need to upload some personal information to purchase a digital asset. With the modern systems, there is a trade-off that needs to be done with some of your anonymity. However, the benefits when it comes to security are worth it.

Still, once you are invested with some gains, you can send your funds to a decentralized exchange and enjoy confidentiality.

Regarding where you should store your cryptocurrency, it may be in your best interest to send your funds to a hardware wallet or cold storage if you're not actively trading your funds or keeping them in a stable coin for immediate purchases. One suitable option for a hardware wallet is the Ledger Nano X. It stays offline until you're making a transaction, significantly lowering the probability of your funds being hacked. It makes sense if your wallet is "cold" when you are not actively using it. It means no one can mess with it while you are asleep. No more panicking in the mornings and checking your wallets to see if your savings are still intact. It would take a hacker coming to you physically and taking your passcode for them to take your crypto (and by that point, you might have to worry more about your physical security than your virtual one). Jokes aside, it has become much simpler and easier to prevent your crypto from getting stolen, and technology like this is the way forward.

Hardware wallets come with 12 or 24-word seed phrases that you need to input to recover your funds. It is essential to keep these phrases safe. Losing these phrases will ultimately result in the permanent loss of your funds.

So, it is better to have these backed up physically on a ledger or diary just for safe-keeping. It is all well and good to have your savings safe, but if even you can not access your funds, then there is no point in having a wallet!

To finish up this chapter, before using any exchange, please verify that it has been used and verified by other users. This is true for most anything, especially in the finance world, but it would not be prudent to have money tied up in shady exchanges. Always trade and do business with known interactions trusted and verified by many people and other individuals involved in this world.

Chapter 6: Trading

In the context of crypto-currencies, the best way to make money is to take a financial position on whether a particular asset will go up or down in value against the dollar or another currency. Where an investor will do this in the long term, buying to keep and waiting to sell when the price rises, a trader looks to do this in the short term.

This can be done by predicting a currency will go up and buying some of it today, or in the form of short-term trades like day-trading. Whatever the case, trading in crypto-currency is like placing a bet on whether or not the value of a particular asset will rise or fall over a given time. This could be done in responsible or irresponsible ways, so this chapter will try and push you to trade in the best manner.

You analyze and predict whether or not, in a set amount of time, the price of a particular currency will increase or decrease in a specified period. The best of this kind of trading is called technical trading, where a lot of analytical work goes into deciding if a currency will gain or lose its value over the next cycle (period). Instead of guessing if Bitcoin, for example, will go up or down, you would look at existing trends and data points to enforce your prediction. For this, you will need to understand the types of charts most helpful in making these analyses.

The most common type of chart you will come across is a line chart. A line chart represents an asset's historical price action by connecting data points with a continuous line. This is the most basic type of chart used in finance, showing the assets closing prices over time. You might have seen many examples of line charts in pop culture, which are the easiest to understand.

Charts that show price action can be viewed at any time frame for the most part. For example, the price action of an asset can be viewed on a smaller time frame, such as the 5-minute chart, which shows the price action of an asset every 5 minutes up to a monthly or yearly chart. The most practical use of this feature would be observing day-to-day price changes significantly as a long-term investor because intraday price action can distract you from the overall bigger picture. If you are trading and zoom in too much, you might place your bets on a currency going up or down based on little spikes and shifts rather than on trends.

Day trading is buying and selling an asset within a single trading day. This can occur on many marketplaces such as foreign exchanges (forex), stock markets, and crypto exchanges. Day traders are typically well versed in technical and fundamental analysis and are well funded with education in trading. Traders can use different amounts of leverage or purchase spot prices to capitalize on price movements in highly liquid assets.

Technical analysis (T.A.) is a trading discipline used to evaluate investments by charting. The goal is to find the best trading opportunities in trending prices and patterns. Traders believe that past trading activity and security price changes can be valuable indicators of the security's future price movements. T.A. can be used in any security with historical trading data, including cryptocurrencies, stocks, futures, commodities, fixed-income, currencies, etc. The most popularly used is forex.

Typically, a person using technical analysis looks at:

- Price Trends – The overall direction of a market or an asset's price.

- Chart Patterns – Distinctive formations created by the movements of security prices on a chart.

- Volume and Momentum Indicators –Measure the rate at which the price of a specific stock fluctuates.

- Oscillators – Technical analysis tools construct high and low bands between two extreme values.

- Moving Averages – A calculation used to analyze data points by creating a series of averages of different subsets of a complete data set.

- Support and Resistance Levels – Price points on a chart where the probabilities favor a pause or reversal of a prevailing trend.

- Support – Occurs when a downtrend is expected to pause due to a concentration of demand.

- Resistance – Occurs when an uptrend is expected to pause due to a supply concentration temporarily.

Technical analysis is contrasted with fundamental analysis (F.A.), which focuses on a company's financials rather than historical price patterns or stock trends. Fundamental analysis determines a stock's "real" or "fair" market value.

Fundamental analysts search for stocks currently trading at higher or lower prices than their actual value. F.A. is a method of measuring a security's intrinsic value by examining related economic and financial factors. Fundamental analysts study anything that can affect the security's worth, from macroeconomics factors, such as the state of the economy and industry conditions to microeconomic factors like the effectiveness of the company's management. This is usually done from a macro to micro perspective to identify securities that are not correctly priced by the market. This is much harder to do in the crypto-world where the factors that affect price changes are much more difficult to determine than, say, a regular corporation's shares.

There are many different trading styles, such as scalping, range trading, swing trading, news-based trading, etc. Every trading style is unique and different similar to how people prefer different trading methods.

My best advice would be to expose yourself to all methods and find out what works best for you while utilizing proper risk management. It is strongly recommended to risk 1% of your total portfolio in day trading, but this all depends on your risk tolerance.

In our opinion, the style of trading with the least amount of overall risk exposure is simply buying and holding (HODL) for the long term, whatever the asset. This method can be utilized by looking at a chart for the best buying potential opportunities, commonly known as "buying the dip," or using a chart for potential take profit opportunities. A primary passive investing strategy is simply dollar-cost averaging (D.C.A.) into an asset. When utilizing the D.C.A. method, you invest a set amount of money into an asset regardless of the market price. This way, you can minimize the time you spend administering your portfolio, which can be applied to all securities and digital assets.

Don't forget one of the most important things about trading—profit-taking!

Profit-taking is selling a security or asset to lock in gains. While the process benefits the investor taking the profits, it can also hurt other investors because every seller needs a buyer, and every buyer needs a seller, thus creating price change. Whatever your reason for profit-taking, you should have one.

Whether that reason is a stock or digital asset moving to a specific price target or simply rising sharply in a short period, remember that when and how much you sell will determine what you pay as far as taxes are concerned. And considering that since crypto-trading is a reasonably new phenomenon, the tax regulations and legislation are also adapting to accommodate the industry. This means that keeping an eye on new regulatory measures might be prudent since changes across the short term are much more likely in the following years.

You must remember, however, that playing with risky assets and day-trading without doing your research is much like gambling and poses similar temptations to those with gambling addictions as a casino. Traders that do their research and get into the technical side of things tend to do much better in the long run and always remember to risk only as much as you can afford to lose. Trade safely and responsibly to reap the maximum awards from the world of crypto-trading.

Closing

Congratulations! You are one step closer to fully immersing yourself in cryptocurrency's fun-filled, exciting world! While this may still feel a bit daunting, we believe that referring to this handbook and doing your research will give you a deeper understanding of cryptocurrency and more confidence in investing your time and money into it.

Remember that you control your destiny regarding cryptocurrency, and accountability is critical. Remember that you are the only person that can guarantee your success. As with anything else in life, you can never have too much knowledge of cryptocurrency. Never stop educating yourself. The cryptocurrency universe constantly adapts and adds new things to space, so you must work to stay ahead of the curve.

If this handbook has made you more eager to dive deeper into the world of cryptocurrency, click on the link below to join our monthly membership discord group that will not only teach you how to become a skilled trader, but we will personally work with you one on one to answer all your questions, provide you with hours of videos that will help you learn the basics and be there to walk you through the process every step of the way.

Thank you for taking the time to read our handbook, we hope it served you well, and we look forward to you joining our group and becoming a member of the Honorable Assets Family!

Glossary

2fa – Two Factor authentication is a security measure that requires two methods to verify identity before logging in. You will usually see this on most exchanges to ensure your funds are never at risk of being stolen. The recommended authenticator to use is Google authenticator.

Address – A cryptocurrency address is a unique string of characters where you send and receive crypto assets. Each crypto asset has an individual address that should be double and triple-checked before sending any funds. For example, sending Bitcoin to an Ethereum address will result in a permanent loss of funds.

Alt Coins – altcoins or alternate coins are any cryptos other than Bitcoin. I believe it to be any other coin outside the top 5 on coinmarketcap.com.

APY – Annual Percentage Yield

Bear Market – A market in which prices are falling, encouraging selling

Bull Market – A market in which prices are rising, encouraging buying

Blockchain – A digital ledger that displays transactions for public use. It establishes trust and transparency. It works with a network of computers and miners to verify each transaction without needing a centralized third party.

Crypto Dividends – Interest payments on borrowed cryptocurrency.

D.C.A. – Dollar Cost Averaging

Decentralized – This term simply refers to a currency not controlled by a bank or government system.

Encryption is securing digital data using one or more mathematical techniques and a password or "key" to decrypt the information.

An exchange – is a business or platform that allows customers to trade cryptocurrency for other assets, such as conventional fiat money or other digital currencies.

Fiat – Fiat is money backed by governments instead of physical commodities or a financial instrument.

Fork – This occurs whenever a community changes the blockchain protocol.

F.U.D – Fear, Uncertainty, Doubt

Halving – This is when the rewards miners get are cut in half.

Inflation – This is the decrease in the value of a particular currency caused by the increase in prices in an economy.

Leverage – In a stock transaction, a trader can take on a more significant position in a stock without paying the entire purchase price.

Liquidity – The ability of a coin to be easily converted into cash or other coins.

Market Cap –Market capitalization is a crypto's circulating amount multiplied by the asset's current price. I.E., Bitcoin (at the time of writing) has a circulating amount of 18,955,975 BTC at $42,680 per BTC. The total market cap for BTC is $809,304,155,396.

Metaverse – A virtual-reality space where users can interact with a computer-generated environment and other users.

Mining – Mining is the process of adding new crypto into circulation. Mining is undertaken using sophisticated software to solve complex computational math problems. The first computer to solve these complex problems receives the next block and rewards.

Open Source – Denoting software for which the source code is made freely available and may be redistributed and modified.

Peer to Peer – Relating to, using, or being on a network on which computers operated by individuals can share information and resources directly without relying on a dedicated central server.

Price Action – The movement of a security's price plotted over time. Price action forms the basis for all technical analysis of a stock, commodity, or other asset charts

Rug Pull – A cryptocurrency scam that involves a team pumping their project token and disappearing with the funds

Smart Contracts – Smart contracts are stored on the blockchain that work when predetermined conditions are met.

Spot – The purchase or sale of a foreign currency or commodity for immediate delivery.

Technical Analysis – Financial analysis uses market data patterns to identify trends and make predictions.

Tokens – Units of value that operate on an existing blockchain and can only be used for specific purposes within that environment.

Volatile – Liable to change rapidly and unpredictably, usually for the worse

Wallet – storage for your crypto assets allows you to send and receive. Wallets come in two forms. (Hot) where you hold on an exchange or actively online. Or (cold) where it is held on a physical apparatus and offline until used. A popular cold wallet is a ledger.

Whales – A whale in crypto is a person or entity holding a significant amount of an asset that can cause manipulation if they were to sell.

HONORABLE ASSETS

Made in the USA
Middletown, DE
09 January 2023

21705232R00040